TREASURES
OF THE
TIDE

Lucy Mettler

Nathaniel Eckstrom

ELYON BOOKS

Hardcover: 979-8-9857930-2-4

Printed in the USA.

Elyon Books
3110 Fairview Park Dr., Suite 1300
Falls Church, VA 22042

for my loving grandparents,
Grimble and Tom Tom,
who loved sea treasures
and with whom my time was
cut too short.

Gus woke to the warmth of the sun on his face and the smell of buttermilk and bacon downstairs. Outside, the bluebirds were chirping, their melody baptizing the sunrise in all its glory. Dewdrops bejeweled the blades of grass, glistening as they caught the light.

The family dog, June, leaped onto Gus's bed and began to burrow under the covers.

Mama cooked pancakes on Sundays, and Gus's belly spent every other day of the week grumbling for them. He was carried downstairs by the smell - just like one of the shrimp boats he saw each night being guided into the harbor by the lighthouse.

Gus plopped down at the kitchen table next to his little sister Willa-Mae. She sat happily in her high chair with banana smeared over her face and tangled in her golden curls.

Mama set a stack of pancakes in front of him, the edges perfectly browned and the centers fluffy. Ever since Daddy went to Heaven, she seemed especially tired. But she still managed to be everything a mama ought to be, always putting his and Willa-Mae's well-being first, and never missing a chance for an impromptu game of Tickle Monster.

"Eat quick now," she said. "Pops will be here soon."

On Sundays, Pops took Gus and Willa-Mae to the shoreline. It was their special time together. They strolled in the foamy remnants of the waves, dodging the washed-up jellies and chasing after schools of minnows in the tide pools.

Pops and Gus would engineer the most remarkable drip castles, their fantastical architecture defying the laws of gravity.

But their very favorite game to play had always been shell hunting.

As Mama was clearing the dishes, Pops pulled into the driveway in his sun-bleached blue truck. Gus grabbed his shovel and bucket, and he and Willa-Mae rushed down the front porch steps to greet him.

The beach was fifteen minutes away, and they always kept a prayer-like silence during the drive, anticipating the first signs of the beach. As they got closer, the sounds of seagulls squawking to each other and the smell of salty seabreezes filled the air.

Gus jumped out of the truck and ran through the path that cut across the sand dunes. As he reached the top of the dune, his eyes lit up at the thousands of shells spread out before him.

Pops and Willa-Mae followed behind and selected a spot to plant their beach umbrella. It was noon and the sun was getting higher in the sky.

Gus had always wondered why pirates buried chests of gold instead of chests of shells. Although so many shells are partly broken, he thought, that didn't make them any less beautiful. In fact, it made them beautifully unique. Shells are like fingerprints and snowflakes – no two alike.

God is here, Gus thought. *Who else could make such things?*

He hoped they had infinite shells in Heaven, so Daddy could spend all of eternity wandering along the shore and gathering up the best ones. Gus knew Daddy would save them for him and one day, when they saw each other again, they would bury their favorites in the clouds in a place only the two of them knew how to find.

As Gus surveyed the ocean, a sea urchin emerged from the waves and rolled onto the beach. Gus picked it up, minding its formidable spikes.

He wasn't scared of the spikes, though, because he knew they protected the sea urchin's fragile body. And he knew that underneath the creature's sharp defenses was an intricately formed and beautiful shell.

Holding the sea urchin carefully in his hand, Gus waded into the water and gently placed it back beneath the swells. The sea - not the sand - was its home.

Just beyond where Pops was digging a hole with Willa-Mae, Gus spotted a conch shell nestled in the sand.

Its colors melted into one another - vibrant, shiny hues of pinks and oranges and pearlescent corals.

The conch shell is the Mother of all shells - the Queen of the Kingdom. Gus loved the way it opened up, like it was extending its arms into a hug. He had learned that all kinds of creatures take refuge within her walls, that she is home to tiny snails (called conch), to fish and to crabs.

The conch shell reminded Gus of Mama, how sturdy and strong she was on the outside and how beautiful and colorful she was on the inside.

The waves came and went, taking some shells back to sea and bringing new treasures ashore. Out of the corner of his eye, Gus spotted a White Baby Ear sparkling in the sunlight. It was strikingly white against the dark wet sand.

The White Baby Ear reminded Gus of Willa-Mae - small, pure and innocent. He felt a twinge of jealousy, only for a moment, that she was too young to feel the same sadness he felt about Daddy.

But then Gus realized how fortunate he was to have known Daddy and to be able to remember moments spent with him. And suddenly he didn't feel so jealous of his baby sister.

Next, Gus came across a small colony of angel wing shells, different shades of every color. Some were broken. Others were missing their other half. But when both halves were connected, they truly did look like a pair of wings.

Each time he found angel wing shells at the beach, Gus felt Daddy's presence, as if he were standing right beside him.

Gus tucked the biggest angel wing of the bunch into his hand and walked back to the umbrella to place it in a bucket for safekeeping.

The sun had moved to the west, and the shadow from the beach umbrella was getting longer. Both Gus and Willa-Mae were hungry, so Pops opened the basket of food Mama had sent with them.

Gus sat down to eat his peanut butter and pickle sandwich and ran his feet through the packed sand. The sand beneath was cool to the touch, and his toes bumped into something hard. He dug his feet a little deeper and flicked the object free.

Brushing away the remaining sand, Gus realized to his delight that he was staring into a Cat's Eye.

Of course, it wasn't a real cat's eye - but it looked so much like one that shell collectors gave it this name years ago. This Cat's Eye was a perfect swirl of purple, gray and periwinkle blue. It had a small hole at the top. This would be perfect for a necklace for Mama, Gus thought.

Gus placed the Cat's Eye in a bucket, next to his other
treasures. The tide had continued to recede and had left
a tidal pool close by. The beach and the ocean worked
together to create many gifts - tidal pools included.

Gus belted out to Willa-Mae, "Betcha can't catch me!" and took off running for the tidal pool. Willa-Mae chased after him.

Splash! Willa-Mae lost her balance as she toddled into the shallow water. She reached for the sandy bottom as she tried to stand up and excitedly called out Gus's name.

"Gus Gus! C'mere!" She held out her hand.

"What did you find, Willa-Mae?" Gus asked. She held up her hand for Gus to see.

Gus grabbed the ball of wet sand and dunked it in the water. His palm revealed an ever-so-precious deep sea scallop shell.

The scallop shell had rounded stripes of coral, pink and purple from end to end. Its edges had a few chips, but Gus knew that this was a special find. Gus had read about this type of scallop shell, but he had never found one before.

He grabbed Willa Mae's hand, and they walked back to show Pops.

Pops - one of the best shell collectors Gus knew, second only to Daddy - agreed that it was indeed a beautiful deep sea scallop shell.

"Just think," Pops wondered, "how much ocean that shell has crossed to get here."

Gus could only imagine the journey that this scallop shell had endured on its way to the tidal pool. The chips were part of its story. Without those precise bumps and tumbles it faced through the ocean tides, it may never have ended up in Willa-Mae's hand.

By now, the shadow from the umbrella had grown even longer. The sun was getting closer to where the sky and the ocean meet. The shrimp boats dotted the horizon, on their way back to the docks for a late afternoon docking.

"Time to go, lovies," Pops called. Gus helped Pops pack up. They made their way up the beach and back over the sand dune.

On their way home, Pops cracked the windows of his truck so they could smell the salt air and feel the cool breeze. Gus watched the sweetgrass and brush speed past.

The sun had set, and night was arriving. Gus took his treasures to his room. After rinsing them in the sink, he proudly placed his newfound treasures on the windowsill.

As he climbed into bed and waited for Mama to come tuck him in, Gus thought of Daddy and knew he was looking down and admiring Gus's new additions to his collection.

"You found some true treasures, Gus," he could
almost hear Daddy saying. "I can't wait to see what
you find next."